# Contents

# Introduction

All of the projects in this book are made using polymer clay,
a strong oven-baked clay.

Polymer clay is easy to work with and comes in a wide range of
colours and effects which can all be mixed together. It is lightweight
which makes it perfect for jewellery making but it is also very strong so
it's used for large-scale modelling too. There are very few limits to the
things you can make!

The projects in this book are inspired by Japanese *kawaii* culture.
'Kawaii' means 'cute' in Japanese and has become its own global
culture. There are so many ways to enjoy kawaii, from manga, anime,
fashion and even food! My love for kawaii has led me to create
miniature polymer clay pieces that feature cute, smiling faces.

Taking the knowledge you learn from this book, you'll be well on your
way to starting your kawaii polymer clay journey!

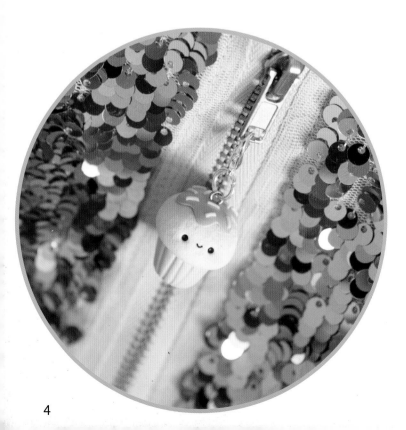

Twenty to **Craft**

# Kawaii Charms
# in Polymer Clay

Ruth Thompson

Search Press

First published in 2021

Search Press Limited
Wellwood, North Farm Road,
Tunbridge Wells, Kent TN2 3DR

ISBN: 978-1-78221-896-8
ebook ISBN: 978-1-78126-890-2

**Publishers' note**
The Publishers and author can accept no
responsibility for any consequences arising
from the information, advice or instructions
given in this publication.

Readers are permitted to reproduce any
of the items in this book for their personal use,
or for the purposes of selling for charity, free
of charge and without the prior permission
of the Publishers. Any use of the items for
commercial purposes is not permitted without
the prior permission of the Publishers.

**Suppliers**
If you have difficulty in obtaining any of
the materials and equipment mentioned
in this book, then please visit the Search Press
website for details of suppliers:
www.searchpress.com

Visit the Twenty to Make website:
www.20toMake.com

You are invited to visit the author's website:
www.kawaiistudios.co.uk
Follow Ruth on Instagram: @kawaii_studios

## Dedication

*This book is dedicated to my incredible parents
who support me in everything I do.*

# Techniques

## Working with polymer clay

The texture of polymer clay varies between brands and finishes but in general it is a firm but workable clay. It will need to be kneaded in your hands to warm it up and make it workable, this process is called 'conditioning'. Some colours of polymer clay may stain so make sure you are working on a mat to protect your work surface.

## Baking polymer clay

Polymer clay needs to be baked to harden, unlike air-drying clays. Each brand of polymer clay will have individual instructions for baking on the packaging. I tend to bake all of my miniature pieces at 110°C for thirty minutes but if you are making larger sculptures, you may have to bake your creations for longer! You can buy specific polymer clay ovens – however, polymer clay is non-toxic and can be baked in a conventional oven. To bake your creations, simply place your polymer clay pieces on a dedicated baking tray lined with baking parchment, and place the tray in the centre of a preheated oven.

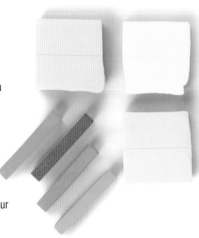

*Above, three blocks of pastel-coloured polymer clay and four chalk pastels for colouring.*

## Tools of the trade

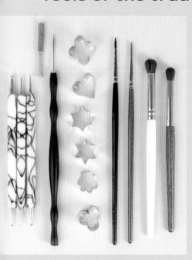

*Above from left to right, dotting tools for texturing and adding faces, shape cutter with plunger, needle tool for adding texture, shape cutters for shaping clay, small paintbrushes and makeup brushes for adding shading to your clay pieces.*

### Dust and dirt

Polymer clay isn't sticky but it will collect any dust or dirt that is on your hands and workspace. To avoid this, make sure you clean your hands thoroughly and wipe your workspace down before starting to craft. Some bright colours will also stain your hands and can transfer to other pieces of clay – make sure to wash your hands in between working with these colours of clay.

### The freezer technique

If you put polymer clay in the freezer for twenty minutes, it will firm up. This technique is very useful when you need to cut something but don't want to lose the shape or texture. It is also helpful if you need to handle it a lot but are worried you will misshape it with your fingers.

## Adding colour to your clay

Adding powder colour to your pieces is a great way to add a bit of realism. Shading is the practice of adding colour to a piece to give it more dimension. For this, you can use any kind of pigment, from chalk pastels or mica pigments to cheap eye shadows. My favourite way to add pigment is with chalk pastels that I have shaved into a powder using a blade – it is an extremely cheap method. I then dust these on my charms using paintbrushes. I use the shading technique to add blush to my faces or to make a food look baked.

# Texturing

Adding texture to some of your pieces adds a lot of depth and dimension. There are lots of different ways to add texture to your polymer clay kawaii miniatures – below are two of my most frequently used techniques and their purposes:

### Fluffy texture

This texture is a multi-tasker – depending on the project you're making, it can look like animal fur or a fluffy cake. Take a needle tool and gently drag it along the surface of the clay in small circular motions; repeat over and over. Depending on how small you make the circles and how hard you press, you will get different results.

### Sponge texture

This is the texture I use for most types of desserts or cakes. To make this sponge texture, all you need is a toothbrush (one that you use only for crafts!). Gently press the bristles into the surface of the clay and repeat this motion to get the desired result.

It's all about experimenting – a lot of these textures can be used for many different things. Get creative and see what things around your house you can use for texturing!

# Adding faces to your pieces

All my kawaii charms feature happy, smiling faces inspired by *manga* and *chibi* art. There are lots of different ways to add faces to your charms. You can use acrylic paint and paint the faces on after baking, you can press glass beads into the clay for eyes or you can use clay to add the faces before baking.

Adding faces can be challenging at first, but practice makes perfect. If you are a beginner, try making your pieces without faces at first to get a feel for polymer clay. You can also start by making the pieces on a bigger scale with bigger faces and with practice you will be able to make them smaller and smaller!

The basic idea is that you use small balls of clay for the eyes and a thin snake of clay for the mouth. My favourite technique is to press two shallow holes in the clay using a small dotting tool for the eyes, place two small balls of clay in those holes, then re-press with the dotting tool. Then I roll out a thin snake of the same clay and place it between the eyes, gently forming it into the correct shape using a dotting tool. If you want to make a kawaii blushing face, you can also do this by pressing balls of clay onto the piece or by using a pink or red shade of chalk pastel and applying it with a small brush.

There are endless ways to make faces and endless expressions. Below are some other ideas – get creative and come up with your own unique styles!

# Finishing your pieces

Instructions for finishing your pieces can be found on page 48.

# Chocolate chip cookie wrist strap

## Materials:

Brown polymer clay

Black polymer clay

Beige polymer clay

Chalk pastels

Eye pin (see page 48)

Ribbon (this should be the same width as the crimp finding)

Ribbon crimp finding (see page 48)

Keychain clip

Glue

## Tools:

Blade

Toothbrush

Pliers

## Instructions:

**1.** Form brown clay into a small rectangle shape no thicker than 10mm (³/₈in).

**2.** Bake this shape for 15 minutes.

**3.** After it has cooled, use a blade to cut it carefully into small chunks – these will be your chocolate chips.

**4.** Mix these chunks of brown clay into a ball of beige-coloured clay and form into a circular dome approximately 20mm (³/₄in) wide and 10mm (³/₈in) tall.

**5.** Add the sponge texture from page 7 using a toothbrush.

**6.** Next, add shading to your cookie by adding a golden yellow chalk pastel colour all over and brown chalk pastels to the outer edge with fluffy brushes.

**7.** Add a face to your cookie using black clay and pink chalk pastels.

**8.** Insert an eye pin into the top of your cookie to create a charm.

**9.** Bake the cookie charm and allow to cool.

**10.** Cut a length of your ribbon that will wrap easily around your wrist. There should be room for you to slide your hand in and out when the ribbon is formed into a loop.

**11.** Add a small amount of glue to the ribbon crimp finding, then place both ends of your ribbon inside and close the crimp using pliers.

**12.** Attach your charm and a keychain clip to the crimp using a jump ring and pliers.

# Doughnut charm bracelet

## Materials:

Beige polymer clay

Pink polymer clay

Mint polymer clay

Brown polymer clay

Chalk pastels

Eye pin (see page 48)

Jump rings (see page 48)

Charm bracelet

## Tools:

Blade

Flower-shaped cutter

Paintbrush

Pliers

## Instructions:

**1.** Form a small amount of beige clay into a ball.

**2.** Flatten to create a disc shape approximately 8mm ($^5/_{16}$in) thick and 15mm ($^9/_{16}$in) wide.

**3.** Taking the end of a thin paintbrush, poke a hole through the centre of the disc to create your doughnut base.

**4.** Then roll out some pink clay into a thin sheet approximately 1mm ($^1/_{16}$in) thick and cut a flower shape out of it using your cutter.

**5.** Place this on the top of the doughnut, making sure to press down the sides. Poke a hole in this sheet of clay in the same place as the base.

**6.** Next, roll some mint-coloured clay into a thin snake and cut it into smaller pieces to create sprinkles. Place these on top of the icing.

**7.** Add a face to the top of the doughnut using brown clay and chalk pastels.

**8.** Add an eye pin to the side of the doughnut above the face.

**9.** Repeat to create more doughnut charms for your bracelet.

**10.** Bake all of the doughnut charms and allow to cool.

**11.** Attach the doughnut charms to a charm bracelet using jump rings and pliers.

### Tip

To make your charms extra durable, add a layer of liquid clay to the icing with a paintbrush and bake for a further fifteen minutes. This will protect the sprinkles and face from any harm during wearing.

# Fried egg earrings

## Materials:

White polymer clay

Yellow polymer clay

Black polymer clay

Eye pin (see page 48)

Fish hook earrings (see page 48)

Jump rings (see page 48)

## Tools:

Blade

Dotting tool

Pliers

## Instructions:

**1.** Taking a ball of white polymer clay, flatten it and shape it into an egg shape approximately 28mm (1¹/₈in) at its widest point and 10mm (³/₈in) thick.

**2.** Form yellow clay into a dome shape for the yolk, approximately 10mm (³/₈in) wide.

**3.** Place this onto the white egg shape.

**4.** Add a face using black clay and chalk pastels.

**5.** Then insert an eye pin into the top side of the egg piece.

**6.** Repeat to create another egg charm for the second earring.

**7.** Bake both egg charms and allow to cool.

**8.** Finally, connect fish hook earring findings to both egg charms using jump rings and pliers.

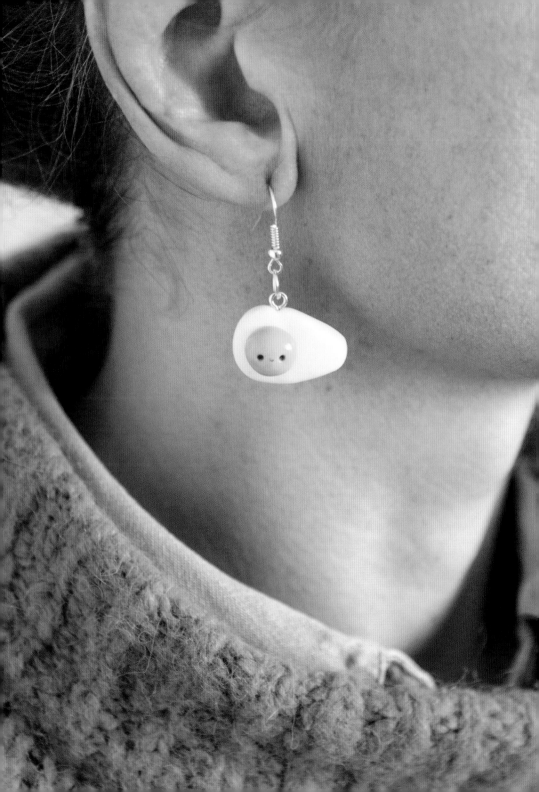

# Sushi earrings

## Materials:

Peach polymer clay

White polymer clay

Black polymer clay

Eye pins (see page 48)

Earring hooks (see page 48)

## Tools:

Blade

Dotting tool

Rolling pin

Pliers

## Instructions:

**1.** Roll out a thick log of black clay and cut two equal cylinders from it.

**2.** Roll them against your surface and press the tops and bottoms between your fingers to create your desired sushi shape. Each shape should be 15mm ($^9/_{16}$in) tall by 70mm (2¾in) long; the base should have a diameter of 15mm ($^9/_{16}$in) across.

**3.** Flatten a ball of white clay into a thin circle that is slightly smaller than the top of the black shape.

**4.** Place this white circle on top of the black shape and press a small dotting tool repeatedly into the surface to create a rice-like texture.

**5.** Then roll out some peach-coloured clay very thinly and cut out a square that will fit inside the white circle.

**6.** Roll out some thin snakes of white clay and place these at even intervals on the peach square.

**7.** Use your rolling pin to gently roll the square shape again to incorporate the white lines. Recut the square shape so the edges are neat again.

**8.** Place this piece on top of the sushi.

**9.** Add a face using clay and a dotting tool.

**10.** Repeat for the other earring and bake both charms allowing them to cool.

**11.** Then add jump rings to the charms and attach them to your earring hooks using pliers.

*There are so many different types of sushi rolls – my favourite is cucumber maki. I used green clay and chalk pastels to make this variation on the salmon rolls.*

# Cupcake charm

## Materials:

Pink polymer clay

Beige polymer clay

Purple polymer clay

Mint polymer clay

Eye pin (see page 48)

Lobster clasp (see page 48)

## Tools:

Blade

Flower-shaped cutter

Toothbrush

Needle tool

Pliers

## Instructions:

**1.** Form a small ball of pink clay into a cone shape, flatten the top and bottom by pressing onto a flat surface. It should be approximately 15mm ($^9/_{16}$in) at its widest and 10mm ($^3/_8$in) high.

**2.** Using a needle tool, press the edge of the needle against the side of the cone shape to create shallow indents. Start by adding four lines evenly spaced around the circumference of the shape.

**3.** Then repeat the process filling in the spaces with two more lines between the four lines you previously made, creating the look of a cupcake case.

**4.** Then form a dome shape using a ball of beige polymer clay approximately 18mm ($^3/_4$in) wide and 18mm ($^3/_4$in) tall.

**5.** Add the sponge texture from page 7 using a toothbrush.

**6.** Next, add shading by brushing a golden yellow coloured chalk pastel all over the shape, then a light brown colour lightly to the centre using fluffy brushes. This makes the cupcake look nice and baked!

**7.** Attach this dome shape to your cupcake base by pressing them gently together.

**8.** Add a face to the top of the cupcake using brown clay and chalk pastels.

**9.** Roll out some purple clay into a sheet 1mm ($^1/_{16}$in) thick and cut a flower shape from it using a cutter.

**10.** Pull and pinch this shape with your fingers to make it less perfect and then place this on top of the cupcake to make icing.

**11.** Next, roll some mint-coloured clay into a thin snake and cut it into smaller pieces to create sprinkles. Place these on top of the icing.

**12.** Insert an eye pin in the top of your cupcake.

**13.** Bake and allow to cool before adding your lobster clasp using a jump ring and pliers.

### Tip

To get a neater-looking charm, cut off the top of the cupcake base using a blade, before attaching to the rest of the cupcake. If this is tricky because the clay is too soft, place the base in the freezer for twenty minutes to firm it up and then cut it.

*The colour combinations and sprinkle choices are endless for this project. You could also use brown clay for the cake to suggest chocolate instead of vanilla!*

# Panda paperclip

## Materials:

Black polymer clay
White polymer clay
Metal paperclip

## Tools:

Blade
Dotting tool

## Instructions:

**1.** Make a ball using white polymer clay and form it into a flat oval shape approximately 7mm (¼in) thick and 20mm (¾in) wide.

**2.** Cut a shallow opening at the base of the oval using a blade.

**3.** Push the top of a metal paperclip into the opening and reform the oval around it so the paperclip is secure.

**4.** Then make two even balls using black clay. Flatten these on your work surface to create discs that are approximately 7mm (¼in) wide.

**5.** Cut a small portion off the bottom of both black discs to allow you to attach them more easily to the white shape. These will be the ears.

**6.** Press the ears gently onto the top of the oval shape to create the panda's head.

**7.** Take some more black clay and create two small even balls and flatten them into ovals.

**8.** Press the ovals onto the front of the panda head.

**9.** Then flatten a small ball of white clay inside the black ovals.

**10.** Add a face to the panda head, putting the eyes in the white circles you just created.

**11.** Bake and allow to cool before use.

*You can make this project super kawaii by using pastel colours, or colours that match your favourite notebook.*

# Sloth peg

## Materials:

Light brown polymer clay
Dark brown polymer clay
Black polymer clay
Tan polymer clay
Wooden peg
Glue

## Tools:

Blade
Dotting tool
Needle tool

## Instructions:

**1.** Make a ball using light brown polymer clay and form it into a flat oval shape 7mm (¼in) thick and 20mm (¾in) wide.

**2.** Take a needle tool and texture it using the fluffy texture technique shown on page 7.

**3.** Create another oval shape approximately 1mm (¹/₁₆in) thick and 18mm (¾in) wide out of tan clay.

**4.** Roll out two balls of dark brown clay and create small oval shapes. Place them on the sides of the larger oval.

**5.** Add a face to this piece using black clay, putting the eyes in the ovals you just made and adding a small oval for a nose.

**6.** Carefully place the oval shape with the face on it on the front of the light brown textured piece.

**7.** Bake and allow to cool.

**8.** Once cool, attach it to your wooden peg using a strong adhesive.

*These pegs are perfect for hanging pictures on string; you can make the sloths in a rainbow of colours too!*

# Cat ring

## Materials:

Black polymer clay

White polymer clay

Orange polymer clay

Pink polymer clay

Chalk pastels

Ring finding (see page 48)

Glue

## Tools:

Blade

Dotting tool

Circle cookie cutter

## Instructions:

**1.** Make a ball using white polymer clay and form it into a flat oval shape approximately 7mm (¼in) thick and 20mm (¾in) wide – this will be the cat's head.

**2.** Then add a face to the centre of the oval using black clay and chalk pastels; this will make it easier to position things.

**3.** Roll out some orange clay no thicker than 1mm ($^1/_{16}$in) and cut a circle using a cutter.

**4.** Lay a portion of this circle on the top left of the oval and cut off any excess clay.

**5.** Next, take a ball of orange clay and a ball of white clay and form them into thick triangles with your fingers. Each side of the triangle should be even and approximately 7mm (¼in) long. These will be the cat's ears.

**6.** Roll out a thin sheet of pink clay and cut out two small triangles: these should be smaller than the ears.

**7.** Place them onto the ear triangles and cut off a small portion of this shape so that you have a flat edge. Attach the ears onto the top of the cat head using this edge.

**8.** Bake the cat head and allow to cool.

**9.** Finally, use a strong adhesive to attach the ring finding to the back of the clay piece.

*These make great gifts for friends and family because you can recreate their own furry friends as pieces of wearable jewellery!*

# Moon and stars keyring

## Materials:

Silver polymer clay

Sparkly yellow polymer clay

Black polymer clay

Gloss varnish (see page 48)

Eye pin (see page 48)

Jump rings (see page 48)

Keyring finding (see page 48)

## Tools:

Blade

Dotting tool

Needle tool

Pliers

Star cookie cutter

## Instructions:

**1.** Take a ball of silver clay and use your hands to form it into a crescent moon shape.

**2.** Using a dotting tool, create a few shallow indents on the top of this shape – these will be the craters.

**3.** Taking very small balls of silver clay, add these to the top of the moon next to the previous indents. Using a small dotting tool, indent the centres of these balls of clay.

**4.** Now add a face using black clay.

**5.** Insert an eye pin in the top of the moon.

**6.** Roll out some sparkly yellow polymer clay 4mm ($^3/_{16}$in) thick and cut a star shape using your cutter.

**7.** Create a hole in the top of the star with a needle tool. Repeat this to create a second star charm.

**8.** Bake the moon and the stars and allow to cool.

**9.** Then glaze all of the charms to bring out the sparkle in the clay colours; allow to dry.

**10.** Once the charms have dried, attach them to the keyring finding using jump rings and pliers.

# Toadstool necklace

## Materials:

Red polymer clay

Beige polymer clay

White polymer clay

Black polymer clay

Eye pin (see page 48)

Necklace chain

Jump ring (see page 48)

## Tools:

Blade

Dotting tool

Pliers

## Instructions:

**1.** Form a ball of red clay into a dome approximately 25mm (1in) wide and 15mm ($^9/_{16}$in) tall.

**2.** Next, take some beige clay and form it into a cone shape approximately 15mm ($^9/_{16}$in) tall and 17mm ($^{11}/_{16}$in) at its widest point.

**3.** Cut a small piece off the top of the cone to create a flat surface and attach the top of the toadstool by pressing the two pieces together.

**4.** Add a face to the beige clay using black polymer clay and chalk pastels.

**5.** Then make small balls using white clay and press them thin and flat to create the toadstool spots.

**6.** Add these to the toadstool using your fingers wherever you'd like.

**7.** Next, insert an eye pin to the top of the toadstool. Use a long eye pin so it will go through the cone shape too; this will make the charm more durable.

**8.** Bake the toadstool charm and allow to cool.

**9.** Then add a jump ring to the charm and attach it to a long necklace chain using pliers.

*You can make a matching jewellery set if you make two more toadstools and turn them into earrings!*

# Succulent figure

## Materials:

Green polymer clay
Pink polymer clay
Black polymer clay
Brown polymer clay
Chalk pastels

## Tools:

Blade
Dotting tool
Paintbrush

## Instructions:

**1.** Form a large ball of pink clay into a cone and press onto your surface to create a flat top and bottom. This will be your plant pot. This shape should be approximately 20mm (¾in) tall and 20mm (¾in) at its widest part.

**2.** Add a thin circle of brown clay to the top of the plant pot shape. Use a large dotting tool to create lots of shallow holes to add a soil texture.

**3.** Roll out a sheet of pink clay 2mm (¹/₁₆in) thick and cut a long thin rectangle. Wrap this around the top of the plant pot to create a rim. Cut off any excess clay.

**4.** Add a face to the plant pot using brown clay and chalk pastels.

**5.** Take a small ball of green clay and gently pinch one side with your fingers, then flatten it to create a leaf shape.

**6.** Repeat this multiple times, making sure you have leaves of varying sizes.

**7.** Now add these to the top of the plant pot on the brown clay starting with the largest leaves at the bottom: they should get smaller as you add them near the top.

**8.** Shade the ends of the leaves with a red chalk pastel and a paintbrush. Be gentle so that you don't ruin the shape of your succulent leaves.

**9.** Bake the succulent and allow to cool.

*You can use the plant pot base to make all kinds of succulent and cactus figures – get creative!*

# Cloud brooch

## Materials:

White polymer clay
Black polymer clay
Chalk pastels
Brooch back finding (see page 48)
Glue

## Tools:

Blade
Dotting tool
Scissors
Pencil and paper for the template

## Instructions:

**1.** Draw a template on paper of the shape and size you want your cloud brooch to be. Cut it out carefully using scissors.

**2.** Roll out a sheet of white polymer clay about 4mm (³/₁₆in) thick.

**3.** Place your paper template on top and use a sharp blade to cut around the shape removing any excess clay.

**4.** Using your finger, round the edges of the cloud shape to make them smooth.

**5.** Add a face using black clay and chalk pastels.

**6.** Bake and allow to cool.

**7.** Then add your brooch back finding using a strong adhesive.

*Get creative and try using different clay colours and faces to create brooches for a variety of weathers and moods, like this sad grey cloud.*

# Bookmark

## Materials:

Purple polymer clay

White polymer clay

Red polymer clay (optional)

Black polymer clay

Chalk pastels

Eye pin (see page 48)

Jump ring (see page 48)

Ribbon (same width as the crimp finding)

Ribbon crimp finding (see page 48)

Glue

## Tools:

Blade

Dotting tool

Pliers

Heart cookie cutter (optional)

## Instructions:

**1.** Cut a rectangle block from white clay, approximately 18mm (¾in) wide, 20mm (¾in) long and 7mm (¼in) thick.

**2.** Texture three edges of the block by dragging a blade lightly across the surface to create shallow cuts. These will be your book's pages.

**3.** Then roll out a sheet of purple clay 3mm (⅛in) thick and cut a long rectangle shape. This should be the same height as your white rectangle and long enough to wrap around it, approximately 20mm (¾in) tall and 40mm (1½in) long.

**4.** Gently wrap the purple shape around the three sides of the white block that don't have texture to create the book cover. Cut off any excess with a blade.

**5.** Insert an eye pin in the top of the book pages.

**6.** Next, add a face to the book using black clay and chalk pastels. You can also add little details at this stage to give the book a genre. I've added a small red heart I made using a cookie cutter but this is optional.

**7.** Bake the book charm and allow to cool.

**8.** Cut your chosen ribbon so you have a piece approximately 23cm (9in) long. Finish one end of the ribbon using a flame.

**10.** Add a small amount of glue to a ribbon crimp finding that is the same width as your ribbon. Place one end of your ribbon inside and close the crimp using pliers.

**11.** Then attach your charm to the crimp using a jump ring and pliers.

*There are so many variations you can make for this project – you can create book charms for different genres, like this sad book, or match them to any fun ribbon you find.*

### Safety warning

Please be careful when using a flame at step 8. If you are under the age of 16, please seek adult supervision.

# Pencil charm

## Materials:

Yellow polymer clay

Silver polymer clay

Beige polymer clay

Black polymer clay

Pink polymer clay

Lobster clasp (see page 48)

Jump ring (see page 48)

Eye pin (see page 48)

## Tools:

Blade

Dotting tool

Pliers

## Instructions:

**1.** Roll out a thick log approximately 10mm ($^3$/$_8$in) thick using yellow clay and cut a section that is about 30mm (1$^3$/$_{16}$in) long.

**2.** Roll out a log of pink clay with the same thickness as the yellow one you just made. Cut a piece approximately 8mm ($^5$/$_{16}$in) long and round the edges at one end.

**3.** Gently attach this to one end of the yellow log you made previously to create your pencil shape.

**4.** Next, roll out out a sheet of silver clay approximately 1mm ($^1$/$_{16}$in) thick. Cut a long rectangle that is 4mm ($^3$/$_{16}$in) wide and long enough to wrap around the pencil shape.

**5.** Wrap the silver piece around the pencil where the yellow and pink pieces meet. Cut off excess clay and score it with a blade to give it some texture.

**6.** Insert an eye pin into the top of the pencil.

**7.** Then create a cone shape using a ball of beige clay. The base of the cone should have the same diameter as the pencil.

**8.** Attach this to the other end of the yellow pencil, gently pressing the two pieces together.

**9.** Cut off the top of the cone and replace it with a tiny amount of black clay and form it into a point.

**10.** Add a face in the centre of your pencil with black clay and chalk pastels.

**11.** Bake and allow to cool completely.

**12.** Attach a lobster clasp to the pencil charm using a jump ring and pliers.

### Tip

When you are cutting round shapes, it's easy to ruin the shape. To avoid this, gently roll your clay back and forwards with the force of the blade as you are cutting it so you don't end up with one flat side.

*You can use the same method to make lots of other stationery items, like coloured pencils and pen charms.*

# Paint palette brooch

## Materials:

Beige polymer clay

Various colours of polymer clay

Chalk pastels

Blank brooch pin (see page 48)

Glue

## Tools:

Dotting tool

Needle tool

Blade

## Instructions:

**1.** Flatten a ball of beige clay and mould into a palette shape using your fingers: it should be approximately 25mm (1in) at its widest. It needs to be wide enough to hide the brooch back you are using.

**2.** Create a wooden texture by dragging your needle tool over the surface of the clay, creating long shallow lines.

**3.** Add a face in the centre of the palette using black clay and chalk pastels.

**4.** Then create very small balls of clay in various colours and place them on the paint palette in random positions around the outside of the shape.

**5.** Press a small dotting tool into these balls of clay repeatedly to flatten them – this will give them a paint-like texture.

**6.** Bake your palette and allow to cool.

**7.** Then glue a blank brooch finding to the back of the palette piece.

### Tip

Score the back of the palette with a sharp blade in a criss-cross pattern to create a stronger bond with the glue, making your brooch more durable.

# Love letter necklace

## Materials:

White polymer clay
Red polymer clay
Black polymer clay
Chalk pastels
Necklace chain
Jump ring (see page 48)

## Tools:

Dotting tool
Needle tool
Blade
Heart cutter
Pliers

## Instructions:

**1.** Roll out a sheet of white clay with a thickness of approximately 3mm ($\frac{1}{8}$in).

**2.** Using a blade, cut a rectangle approximately 25mm (1in) wide and 20mm ($\frac{3}{4}$in) high.

**3.** Then, using the side of a needle tool, indent the clay with a triangle connecting the top corners of the rectangle in the middle.

**4.** Indent two more lines connecting the bottom corners of the rectangle to the triangle you just made.

**5.** Using a cutter, cut a heart out of red clay and place this on the tip of the triangle in the centre.

**6.** Add a face using black clay and chalk pastels.

**7.** Next, using a needle or dotting tool, poke a hole in one of the top corners of the envelope.

**8.** Bake your charm and allow to cool completely.

**9.** Attach a jump ring to the hole in the envelope charm using pliers and string it onto a necklace chain.

# Pumpkin planner charm

## Materials:

Orange polymer clay

Green polymer clay

Brown polymer clay

Black polymer clay

Chalk pastels

Eye pin (see page 48)

Jump ring (see page 48)

Keychain

## Tools:

Blade

Needle tool

Dotting tool

Pliers

## Instructions:

**1.** Form a ball out of orange clay and gently press it against a flat surface until it is approximately 20mm (¾in) wide and 10mm (³/₈in) thick.

**2.** Using the edge of a needle tool, indent the top of the pumpkin with two lines down the centre, vertically and horizontally, splitting it into quarters. Then indent two more lines that split the quarters into eighths.

**3.** Extend each of these lines all the way around the curve of the ball to the bottom to create the indents of the pumpkin.

**4.** Once all the lines have been added, create a shallow hole on the top of the pumpkin where the lines meet.

**5.** Add a very small log of brown clay in the hole you just made to create a stalk.

**6.** Take a very small amount of green clay: roll it into a tapered cone and then flatten it to create a leaf shape; add this next to the stalk.

**7.** Add a face using black clay and chalk pastels.

**8.** Add an eye pin to the top of the charm.

**9.** Bake and allow to cool.

**10.** Attach a keychain to the charm using a jump ring and pliers.

# Christmas bauble ornament

## Materials:

Metallic red polymer clay

Silver polymer clay

Black polymer clay

Jump ring (see page 48)

Eye pin (see page 48)

Ribbon

Gloss varnish (see page 48)

## Tools:

Blade

Needle tool

Pliers

## Instructions:

**1.** Create a ball of red clay approximately 17mm ($^{11}/_{16}$in), using your hands.

**2.** Then make a disc of silver clay by pressing a small ball of it against a flat surface. It should be approximately 10mm ($^3/_8$in) wide and 5mm ($^3/_{16}$in) thick.

**3.** Add texture to the sides of the disc by pressing a needle tool against it to create shallow indentations.

**4.** Gently attach the disc to the top of the ball being careful not to squish the bauble shape.

**5.** Add a face using black clay and chalk pastels.

**6.** Then gently push an eye pin into the top, through the silver disc and the ball.

**7.** Bake and allow to cool completely.

**8.** Then glaze it to bring out the sparkle in the clay colours; allow to dry.

**9.** Attach a jump ring to the eye pin using pliers and string a piece of ribbon through it. Tie a knot in the ribbon to create a loop.

*You can make these baubles in all your favourite festive colours.*

# Christmas pudding ornament

## Materials:

Brown polymer clay

White polymer clay

Red polymer clay

Green polymer clay

Black polymer clay

Eye pin (see page 48)

Jump ring (see page 48)

Ribbon

## Tools:

Dotting tool

Blade

Flower cutter

Pliers

## Instructions:

**1.** Form a pudding shape by rolling a ball of brown clay on one side, then turn it 90 degrees and press it onto a flat surface. Repeat this until you have your desired shape, approximately 20mm (¾in) tall and 20mm (¾in) at its widest part.

**2.** Once your shape has been created, add texture by gently pressing a larger dotting tool into the clay's surface, creating shallow bumps.

**3.** Then roll out a thin sheet of white clay and cut a flower shape using your cutter.

**4.** Place this on the top of your pudding and press down the edges to create the icing.

**5.** Push an eye pin through the top of the pudding.

**6.** Next, form two very small balls of red clay and add them to the top next to the eye pin. Poke a shallow hole in the centres to create berries.

**7.** Taking green clay, roll it into a ball and use your fingers to pinch one end and then flatten it, creating a leaf shape.

**8.** Repeat for the second leaf and add these next to the berries on top of the pudding.

**9.** Then add a face using white and black clay.

**10.** Bake and allow to cool completely.

**11.** Attach a jump ring to the eye pin using pliers and string a piece of ribbon through it. Tie a knot in the ribbon to create a loop.

# Cauldron necklace

## Materials:

Black polymer clay

Green polymer clay

White polymer clay

Pink polymer clay

Eye pin (see page 48)

Necklace chain

Jump ring (see page 48)

## Tools:

Blade

Dotting tool

Pliers

## Instructions:

**1.** Using your hands, form a ball using black clay.

**2.** Press the ball on your surface to create a flat top and bottom. This shape should be approximately 17mm ($^{11}/_{16}$in) wide and 17mm ($^{11}/_{16}$in) thick.

**3.** Form a small amount of green clay into a ball and flatten to create a thin disc. The disc should be 1–2mm ($^{1}/_{16}$in) smaller in diameter than the black clay shape from step 1.

**4.** Place this green disc on top of the black shape.

**5.** Now make a snake of black clay approximately 2mm ($^{1}/_{16}$in) wide.

**6.** Place this around the top circumference of the cauldron shape to cover the edge of the green clay, creating the lip of your cauldron.

**7.** Add very small balls of green clay in random spots on the top to look like boiling bubbles.

**8.** Then add a face using white and pink clay.

**9.** Push your eye pin into the top of the cauldron and bake.

**10.** Once cooled, attach the charm to a necklace chain using a jump ring and pliers.

# Troubleshooting

### Clay too hard?

If you find that your polymer clay has become hard and unworkable, you can use a polymer clay softener or plain petroleum jelly to make it softer. Simply add a small amount of the chosen softener to the clay and condition it with your fingers.

### Clay too soft?

If you find that your clay is too soft, you may need to remove some of the excess oil from the clay. This process is called 'leaching' and you can do it very simply by pressing your clay flat between two pieces of paper and leaving for thirty minutes to one hour. You will find that when you come back, the paper has absorbed the excess oil. Make sure to leave it on a covered surface, as the oil can stain!

# Finishing your polymer clay pieces

Once you have made your polymer clay pieces, you can stop there – or you can add varnishes and glazes. These are clear paint-like substances that can achieve different looks when dry: for example, a gloss varnish will make your charm shiny, whereas a satin will leave it looking semi-matte. These can be used to enhance the effect of your clay – you can use a gloss varnish on sparkly clay, for example. Glazes and varnishes also make your pieces more durable and protect any added elements like paint or shading.

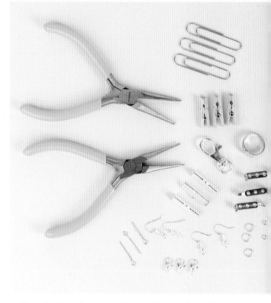

### Making charms from your pieces

The fundamental idea with all these projects is that you turn your pieces into charms to be attached to anything from book marks to necklaces. You can do this by pushing a loop finding into the clay before baking. You can use either eye screws or eye pins for this. I add a small amount of liquid clay to the end of the finding before pressing it in to act as a glue: this will make your charm stronger and less likely to break.

To attach the finished charm to your other findings you will need to use a jump ring. You will need two flat-nosed pliers to work with jump rings. Simply hold the jump ring in the pliers at opposite ends of the opening and pull them away from each other. Then slide on whichever finding you choose and close the jump ring the same way in which you opened it.

*Above: jewellery pliers, paper clips, wooden pegs, keychain clasp, keyring, ribbon crimps, brooch backs, eye pins, fish hook earrings, jump rings and lobster clasps.*

## Acknowledgements

*A special thank you to my followers and friends in the crafting community. Sharing my work with you is an absolute joy and without you this book would not have been possible. Thank you!*

*This pumpkin charm is attached by opening a jump ring using pliers, attaching it to a keychain and then closing the jump ring.*